Soon to Be

Ex-Wife Cookbook

Instead of having an affair,
which hurts the spirit, lets have fun with food!

Doris Garrett   Linda Meighan

ISBN: 978-1-64945-399-0   (Paperback Edition)
ISBN: 978-1-64945-397-6   (Hardcover Edition)
ISBN: 978-1-64945-398-3   (E-book Edition)

Some characters and events in this book are fictitious. Any similarity to real persons, living or dead, is coincidental and not intended by the author.

Book Ordering Information

Phone Number: 347-901-4929 or 347-901-4920
Email: info@globalsummithouse.com
Global Summit House
www.globalsummithouse.com

Printed in the United States of America

Always take care of your Heart.

It belongs to you.

With that comes great responsibility.

Forward

Linda and Doris met in the South Bay at the beautiful Sunflower Nursery where Linda talks about herbs, tea and health habits. After Linda's talk, Doris called Linda and asked if they could work together.

Their theme is: "Herbs are the Companion of the Soul".

A new journey began. Linda and Doris created teatime videos, talked at events together and empowered people in all walks of life.

Their main "office" is on the beach where they go into deep discussion, uplifting themes, new ideas and lots of laughter.

Doris and Linda decided to write a book for the good hearted, wonderful, independent woman with a great sense of humor.

We wish you a fabulous time with this cookbook.

With loving thoughts,

Doris and Linda

*We are so grateful to our family and friends
who supported us while writing this book.*

*And we are grateful to the Chefs who inspired us
to be creative in the kitchen.*

Thank you!

If you use the recipes for revenge,

you need your choice of Dog treats,
Cat food and Fish flakes.

You can grind the dog or cat food to a powder and/or crumble and store in nice jars (with coded labels) and add while you are baking or cooking.

The best revenge is living well with a pinch of
"Soon to be Ex-wife Cookbook"

Contents

Ex-wife stands for: ex-girlfriend, ex-boyfriend, ex-lover,
ex-fiancé, ex-husband, ex-partner, ex-cetra…

HELPFUL HINTS:

Herbs and spices in the kitchen:

Castor Oil for wrinkles: Before going to bed, gently rub castor oil over eyelashes to darken eyelashes and gently around your eyes to help prevent wrinkles.

Cayenne Pepper powder: Before you go for that cold morning walk/run on the beach or in the snow, sprinkle a little cayenne pepper powder in your socks to keep your feet warm and dry. If you are sensitive to peppers, test out a bit of cayenne on your feet first.

*Also, mix cayenne with corn starch to turn the mix into a foot dryer and foot warmer. Mix ½ teaspoon of cayenne powder with 2 tablespoons of corn starch. Sprinkle a teaspoon into each sock and scrunch the sock a bit to distribute the powder evenly before putting your foot in and you're off!

Cloves: toothache tamer- slightly mash a dried clove and hold against tooth.

Thyme: muscle relaxer and joint pain- Put a small bunch of thyme into a warm bath

Fennel: breath freshener- for example, after a meal with garlic pass a bowl of fennel for guests to chew on

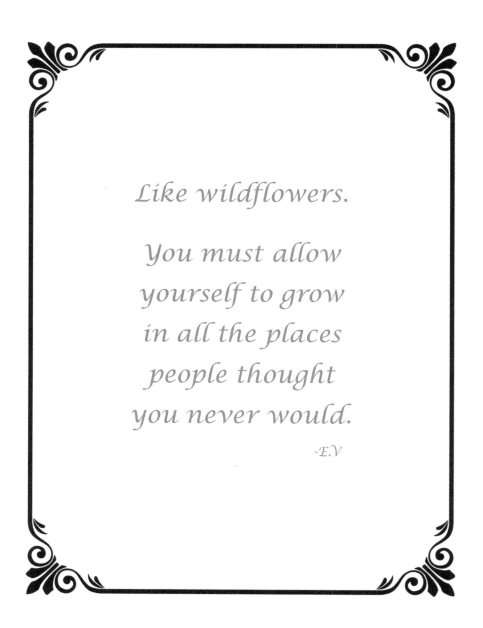

Like wildflowers.

You must allow
yourself to grow
in all the places
people thought
you never would.

-E.V

Affirmation:

Today I focus on thoughts that make me smile.

I fill my mind with uplifting and positive thinking.

I enjoy this day.

The Universe loves and supports me.

Breakfast

Repeat after me:

I have the Courage

To Believe in Myself!

Now it's time to start the morning
and have a great day!

... and then coffee:

My Non-Coffee Drink (makes 1 large or 2 small servings)

1 cup almond milk
¾ cup water
2 Medjool dates
2 heaping tablespoons of your favorite coffee substitute
3 tablespoons almond butter
1 teaspoon fresh peeled ginger
⅛ teaspoon clove
⅛ teaspoon nutmeg
¼ teaspoon cinnamon
1 teaspoon vanilla

Blend and Enjoy!

Be with someone
that makes
YOU happy.

Unknown

Healthy Drink

Detox in the Morning

2 tablespoons apple cider vinegar
1½ tablespoons fresh lemon juice
add cinnamon, to taste
1 tablespoon honey, optional
1 glass of room temperature water

Great Benefits:

Energy
Body Detoxification
Lose Weight
Appetite Control

Banana Muffins

3 medium ripe bananas, mashed
½ cup almond milk
¼ cup coconut oil, melted
2 teaspoons vanilla
½ cup brown coconut sugar
1¼ cup Spelt flour
½ cup old-fashioned rolled oats
1 teaspoon baking powder
½ teaspoon baking soda
½ teaspoon cinnamon
1 pinch sea salt
1 tablespoon apple cider vinegar

To get that feeling of satisfaction and joy for that loving moment of revenge, add a few pinches of ground cat treat.

Preheat oven to 350 degrees F and lightly grease a standard 12-hole muffin tin.

In a bowl, mash or blend: bananas, milk, oil, vanilla and brown coconut sugar.

In a separate bowl, whisk together: flour, oats, baking powder, baking soda, cinnamon and sea salt.

Combine the wet and dry ingredients.

Stir in vinegar.

Bake in preheated oven for 25-30 minutes. Insert toothpick in center to make sure center comes out clean. Cool muffins on wire rack for about 5 minutes; then take out of pan and let cool completely.

Affirmation:

\

I am feeling joyful, fabulous and dynamic!

I will fill my mind with great new positive thoughts.

I give myself permission to shine.

When people are intimidated
by your strength
and happiness,
they'll try to tear
you down,
and break your spirit.
Remember,
it is a reflection
of their weakness,
and not a reflection of you.

Social Media

Live your Life

We often focus too much on what is happening to us instead of what is happening with us -inside of us.

Many times, we don't let go and we feel stuck.

How do we approach a challenging situation? What do we feel? How is our body reacting?

We need to understand that our true Self never changes.
Do you know who you are? You are a most amazing soul in your body. You are wonderful and fabulous. Nobody has your fingerprint. You are unique. There is no one like you. If you don't live your life – who will? You are here to experience life. By understanding this, you will be comfortable with the changes in your life, then you can face challenges with confidence.

We are here to learn more about ourselves.
When you find selflove and self-acceptance, you cannot harm anyone if you understand that feeling. You can choose how you feel. This is your power!

So, I ask you: What will you do with this life? Look at what other people do to you, or work on yourself? Love yourself and know, if you have a bad moment, this is your moment to change and create something better.

How do you feel better? Listen to your favorite music, go for a walk, write in a journal, call a friend, write down all the things you are grateful for... Look at the good things in your life. Focus only on things that make you feel positive. Feel your power!

There are no accidents in the universe. We are here at this moment, in this place and in this body to live our lives.

Never forget who you really are!

Affirmation:

I embrace Life!

It is a wonderful day to count my blessings.

I am free and independent.

I am a wonderful person and I shine through the day.

I accept happiness and I deserve to live in an atmosphere of love and joy.

"Quickie" Pancakes

Combine:

1 very ripe banana
1 egg (or egg substitute)
2 tablespoons Spelt flour

To get that feeling of satisfaction and joy for that loving moment of revenge, add a few pinches of ground cat treat.

Makes 2 pancakes!

"Aquaman" Quiche

1 frozen pie crust, bake and set aside
1 teaspoon oil
½ onion, sliced into thin strips
1 red pepper, sliced into thin strips
1 teaspoon minced garlic
½ lb. mushrooms, chopped
2 cups loosely packed spinach
1½ cups milk or nut milk of choice
5 eggs or equivalent egg substitutes
¼ teaspoon sea salt
¼ teaspoon pepper
⅛ teaspoon nutmeg
½ cup grated cheese or vegan cheese of choice

To get that feeling of satisfaction and joy for that loving moment of revenge, add a few pinches of fish flakes.

Preheat oven to 350 F.

Heat oil in a medium size pan. Sauté onions and peppers for 2-3 minutes. Add mushrooms and garlic and cook until mushrooms are cooked through, about 5 minutes. Add spinach and cook 1 minute longer. Remove pan from heat and set aside.

Crack eggs and whisk until frothy. Add milk, salt, pepper, and nutmeg and whisk in.

To keep crust from getting soggy, remove any excess liquid from the cooked veggies by gently squeezing them in a cheese cloth over the sink.

Place veggies in crust in an even layer. Sprinkle cheese on top. Then pour egg mixture evenly over the veggies and cheese.

Bake for 40-45 minutes until starting to brown on top. Remove from oven and let sit for 10 minutes before cutting and serving.

Apple Cinnamon Quinoa Bowl

½ cup quinoa
1½ cups water
2 medium apples, peeled and chopped
2 teaspoons cinnamon
2 tablespoons walnuts or pecans, chopped
maple syrup or honey, to taste

To get that feeling of satisfaction and joy for that loving moment of revenge, add a few pinches of ground cat treat.

Add quinoa, water and apples to a saucepan. Bring to a boil, cover and reduce to simmer for 20 - 25 minutes. The apples will be soft, and the quinoa will have absorbed the water.

Stir in cinnamon.

Add nuts and drizzle with maple syrup or honey and sprinkle with additional cinnamon, if desired.

Enjoy!

Lemon Verbena Ritual

Uplifting and Relaxing

Take a leaf from a Lemon Verbena plant.

Inhale...Exhale... while holding the leaf in your fingers thank the plant for her gift. Feel the amazingness of the leaf. Be in the moment.

Inhale...Exhale...

Smell that wonderful fragrance from this one leaf. It surrounds you with sweetness and harmony.

Inhale...Exhale...

Take the gift of sweetness and harmony with you throughout the day.

Inhale...Exhale...

Thank the Lemon Verbena plant for her gift and the reminder to be in the moment.

Inhale...Exhale...

Lemon Verbena Tea Ritual

...then take

3 Lemon Verbena leaves and put in

4 cups water and

Boil for 15 minutes

*Chop leaves before boiling for a stronger flavor

Make your own fun Breakfast Recipe

Lunch

For the Green Goddess...

Salad:

Cut up:

(bell peppers) green/yellow/red/orange
tomatoes
broccoli
fuji apples
radishes
walnuts
Lettuce: arugula, baby spring mix or your favorite greens

Toss with fresh lemon juice or use creamy "Green Goddess dressing" (see below)

To get that feeling of satisfaction and joy for that loving moment of revenge, add a few pinches of fish flakes.

Dressing:

1 cup cashews (soaked overnight)
1 cup water
½ teaspoon sea salt
1 teaspoon fresh lemon juice
1 teaspoon minced onion
1 teaspoon garlic powder
⅓ cup fresh basil
⅓ cup fresh dill

Blend all ingredients together. Add more water to desired consistency.

Work on being
in love
with the person
in the mirror
who has been
through so much,
but is still standing.

Unknown

Greek Pasta Salad

2½ cups English or Japanese cucumber, diced
2 cups cherry tomatoes, halved
1 bell pepper (red or orange), diced
½ cup pitted kalamata olives
⅓ cup red onion, diced
½ cup feta cheese, cubed

To get that feeling of satisfaction and joy for that loving moment of revenge, add a few pinches of ground dog treat.

Dressing:

¼ cup raw cashews (soaked for ½ hour)
2 tablespoons fresh lemon juice
4 tablespoons water
1 teaspoon dried oregano
1 teaspoon garlic powder
½ teaspoon sea salt
3 tablespoons apple cider vinegar

Serve on 16 oz. noodles of your choice or even "zoodles"

Quick Chili

(1) 15 ounce can each: black/ kidney/ great northern beans
(Rinse really, really, really well...)
(1) 15 ounce can, diced tomatoes
(1) 8 ounce can tomato sauce
1 small to medium onion
½ each of bell peppers: green/red/yellow/orange
1-2 cups water, to desired consistency
Your favorite taco seasoning
Braggs Aminos (salt substitute), to taste
Add, cayenne pepper for a nice jolt!!!

To get that feeling of satisfaction and joy for that loving moment of revenge, add a few pinches of ground dog treat.

Put all ingredients in crock pot and go about your daily routine

REMEMBER: this is basic, you can add whatever you would like

Healing your Emotions

When you have negative emotions like anger, hurt, or regret…don't fight, or numb them with alcohol, food, drugs …

This emotion that feels so hurtful is a part of you. You need to rescue it. This is a part of your inner self. Pain is something that needs to be acknowledged and processed. The first step is to recognize the pain and honor it by moving our awareness into it.

Healing is a "recovering" or "safe "emotion that shows you were probably hurt a long time ago.

It is important to feel it. If you can feel it, you can heal it.

We think that other people or situations are hurting us. We think it is coming from the outside and we feel powerless. But it is you who are hurt. You feel it, and only you can change it. We are not powerless at all. We choose our emotions.

You need to heal from the inside out. This is your power.

When you work on yourself, look at your negative emotion, it is an incredible journey to live a better life.

Negative feelings are guiding you to a better relationship with yourself!

If you recover from that emotion, you will become wonderful, whole and healed. You will start to accept all of you, and realize how amazing you really are.

There is only one person who can grant you permission to change your life. I'm guessing you won't be surprised when I tell you … that person is YOU!

Life is in front of you. Not behind you.

Affirmation:

I am wonderful, whole and complete, just as I am.

*I am in loving peace with myself and accept
my responsibilities with joy.*

I am now willing to take the next step.

I love life. I love me.

Never Piss off a Women,

they remember stuff

that hasn't even

happened yet.

Unknown

A fun Trick from Social Media

Ratatouille

2 tablespoons extra virgin olive oil
½ medium red onion
1 red bell pepper, diced
1 orange bell pepper, diced
1 medium zucchini, diced
1 yellow squash, diced
3 garlic cloves, minced
1 large ripe tomato, diced
½ teaspoon sea salt
⅛ teaspoon cayenne pepper

To get that feeling of satisfaction and joy for that loving moment of revenge, add a few pinches of ground cat treat.

Heat oil in large sauté pan over medium-high heat. Cook onion for 2 minutes. Add yellow and orange bell pepper and cook 2 more minutes. Add zucchini and yellow squash and cook for 2 more minutes. Finally add garlic, tomato, salt and 1/8 teaspoon cayenne pepper, cook for 1 minute.

Toss with 16 oz. hot cooked pasta.

Enjoy!

Pizza Crust (no yeast)

1⅓ cups Spelt flour
1 teaspoon baking powder
½ teaspoon sea salt
½ cup water
2 tablespoons olive oil

To get that feeling of satisfaction and joy for that loving moment of revenge, add a few pinches of ground dog treat or fish flakes.

Mix flour, baking powder, and salt together in a bowl; stir in water and olive oil until it forms into a soft dough. Put dough onto a lightly floured surface and knead 10 times. Shape dough into a ball. Cover dough and let sit for 10 minutes.

*If dough is dry add a little more water

Roll dough into a 12-inch circle on a baking sheet.

Bake crust at 400 degrees F for 8 minutes.

*Top crust with your favorite toppings and bake until light golden brown for 15 to 20 minutes.

Good to know:

Any Separation is a very strong emotional feeling
that can keep you from the life you wish to live.
If you feel negative emotion, you can heal it.
This is a chance to get to know yourself better. You can grow.

Stop focusing too much on other people.
You can never control them. Focus on *you*.
Focus on how *you* can heal yourself.

Find tools that work best for you,
so you can start releasing energy from the emotion that kept you stuck.

The purpose of releasing energy is to unlock the molecules of emotion
that have locked the pattern of behavior in that place.

Keep your focus on solutions rather than on problems.

Your Soul wants to expand.

You are here to succeed!

You start to know YOURSELF better.

Gratitude:

Studies have proven that the practice of gratitude
can increase happiness levels by around 25%.

In addition to this, they have found that gratitude brings other health benefits,
such as longer and better quality of sleep.

Gratitude is healthy for us!

The word _Relationship_

was first founded in 1390, meaning "Bringing Back, Restoring".

Bring back love and life to _you_.

The most important relationship is with yourself.
You are with yourself, until the very last day, in this body.

So, how is your relationship with yourself?
How do you talk to yourself?

Be free to do things that _you have_ always wanted to do.

Build your dreams and hopes on _you_.

If you feel excited, there is movement.

There is life inside you and it wants to come out.

Make sure _you_ have the best relationship with _yourself_.

We are responsible for ourselves.

AVOCADO CHICKEN (or TOFU SALAD)

2-3 boneless, cooked and shredded chicken breasts (or 1-16oz. block firm tofu)
2 avocados
¼ purple onion, chopped
juice from ½ of a lime
2 tablespoons cilantro, finely chopped
½ celery stock, finely chopped

To get that feeling of satisfaction and joy for that loving moment of revenge, add a few pinches of ground cat treat.

Mash avocados, then add and mix all ingredients together.

Serve on lettuce wraps, tortilla wraps or as a dip.

ENJOY!

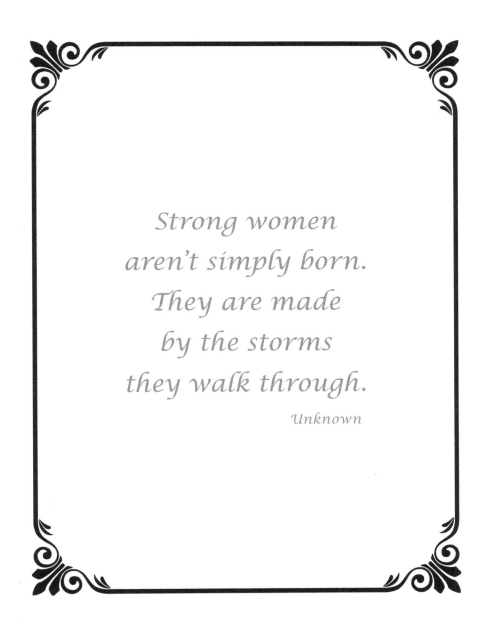

Strong women
aren't simply born.
They are made
by the storms
they walk through.

Unknown

<u>*Did you know...*</u>

"Biting your lip" means to refrain from expressing your feelings;
"Buttoning your lips" or "zippering your lips" means to keep information secret; and
"Keeping a stiff upper lip" means to face adversity courageously

Tampons: In an emergency, you can use two appropriate-sized Tampons as earplugs.

Fiberglass can be of good use if you have an unfaithful husband. Wear gloves and put Fiberglass in his underwear. Be careful with dark underwear. He may see the "Shiny Fiberglass". 😉

"Dreamt" is the only English word that ends in the letters "mt."

Our eyes are always the same size from birth, but our nose and ears never stop growing.

The sentence: "The quick brown fox jumps over the lazy dog" uses every letter of the alphabet.

Teatime inspires kindness, forgiveness …

Using the same teapot can make you feel comfort during solitude and at the same time feel pleasure with company.

Every once in a while, give your partner a little tea and sympathy.

Tea began as a medicine and morphed into a beverage of choice.

As you are sipping on your herbal tea, you can use the same tea bags on the eyes as an inexpensive home remedy. It not only aids relaxation but may also help with several eye ailments, such as:

- Cold chamomile or fennel tea bags are used to help relieve symptoms of pink eye. They may also help to remove excess fluid that is draining from your eye and can also relieve swelling and irritation.

- Warm eyebright, or lavender tea bags on your eyes helps to retain moisture and alleviate dryness. The soothing properties of these teas can relieve any irritation or sensitivities you may be experiencing.

*Since eyes are very sensitive always be careful when using tea bags so here are a few things to keep in mind:

- Never use hot tea bags, always cool first.
- Wash your hands and face thoroughly before treatment.
- Avoid tea bags that contain staples.
- Use unbleached tea bags.
- Keep liquid out of your eyes.
- Remove contacts before doing the treatment.
- Avoid rubbing or touching your eyes.

Affirmation:

I am aware that I can control my happiness.

I am seeing the world with fresh and joyful eyes.

I know that miracles continually occur in my life.

I am special and wonderful.

Make your own fun Lunch Recipe

Dinner

"Classic Wolf" Potato Soup

2½ lbs. potatoes, peeled and diced into 1-inch cubes
4 cups vegetable or chicken stock
½ yellow onion, sliced and sautéed
1 cup canned coconut milk, unsweetened
¼ teaspoon garlic powder
1½ teaspoon sea salt
¼ teaspoon thyme or chives, dried

To get that feeling of satisfaction and joy for that loving moment of revenge, add a few pinches of ground dog treat.

Add stock, onion and potatoes to soup pot. Bring to a boil, then cook for approximately 5-8 minutes or until potatoes are easily pierced with fork.

Once cooked, remove 1 cup of the diced potatoes from stock, set aside.

Blend the stock, sautéed onion and potatoes (excluding the 1 cup that was set aside) and coconut milk until smooth. Pour back in pot and combine all remaining ingredients, including the potatoes that were set aside. Stir.

Put the finished soup into bowls and top with fresh chives or whatever your heart desires.

Cat Women's Spaghetti Recipe

(Slow Cooker / Crock Pot)

1 lb. ground turkey (or shitake mushrooms)
1 tablespoon olive oil
1 large onion, chopped
3 cloves garlic, finely chopped
2 cans (15 oz each) tomato sauce
1 can (28 oz) diced tomatoes
1 can (6 oz) tomato paste
2 tablespoons basil leaves, dried
1 teaspoon oregano leaves, dried
½ teaspoon sea salt
½ teaspoon crushed red pepper flakes

To get that feeling of satisfaction and joy for that loving moment of revenge, add a few pinches of wet cat food.

In 12-inch skillet, heat oil over medium heat.

*Add **ground turkey**, onions and garlic; cook about 10 minutes, stirring occasionally, until turkey is no longer pink. Then spoon into slow cooker/crock pot. Stir in remaining ingredients.

Cover and cook on low heat for 8-9 hours.

*If using **shitake mushrooms** instead of turkey, cook for 4-5 minutes or until onions tender and translucent.

Serve over your favorite pasta.

Affirmation:

I am worthy to attract a high income.

I allow my income to expand.

I attract new, positive and exciting changes in my life.

Amazing and wonderful people enter into my life.

I am open to amazing possibilties in my life.

Sloppy Joe

1 medium carrot, finely chopped
1 stalk celery, finely chopped
½ medium onion, finely chopped
¼ teaspoon garlic powder
1 tablespoon olive oil
1 lb. ground turkey
1 cup tomato sauce
1 teaspoon apple cider vinegar
1 teaspoon mustard
1 tablespoon honey
¼ teaspoon sea salt (optional)

To get that feeling of satisfaction and joy for that loving moment of revenge, add a few pinches of ground dog treat.

In a large pan over medium heat, sauté the carrots, celery, and onion in olive oil until translucent, about 5-8 minutes.

Add garlic powder and cook for 30 seconds.

Add ground turkey and break it up with a spoon. Increase the heat to medium-high, stirring often, until the turkey is no longer pink.

Add tomato sauce, vinegar, mustard, and honey to the pan. Stir well to combine, then cover and simmer for 5 minutes.

Remove the lid, and simmer five minutes more, uncovered, until the sauce is thick and flavorful. Add salt to taste.   *4-6 hamburger buns

CARROT GINGER SOUP

1 tablespoon extra-virgin olive oil
1 cup onions, chopped
1½ teaspoons fresh ginger, grated
2 heaping cups carrots, chopped
1 tablespoon apple cider vinegar
3-4 cups water
sea salt and black pepper, to taste
½ teaspoon basil
½ teaspoon chives
½ teaspoon parsley
Dollop of whip cream (optional)

To get that feeling of satisfaction and joy for that loving moment of revenge, add a few pinches of ground cat treat.

In a large pot over medium heat, sauté onions and ginger with a pinch of salt and pepper and cook until softened, stirring occasionally, about 5 minutes.

Add chopped carrots to the pot and cook about 5 minutes more, stirring occasionally.

Add apple cider vinegar and 3 to 4 cups of water, depending on desired consistency. Reduce to a simmer and cook for about 30 minutes or until carrots are soft.

Transfer to blender when slightly cool. Add basil, chives and parsley. Blend until smooth. Season to taste and serve with dollop of whip cream.

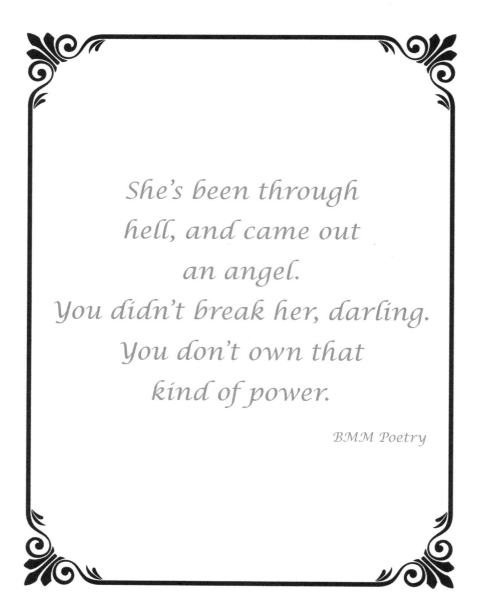

She's been through
hell, and came out
an angel.
You didn't break her, darling.
You don't own that
kind of power.

BMM Poetry

Affirmation:

I now go within me. I let go of the negative emotion.
I am ready to talk lovingly and kindly to myself.

I appreciate my body and take good care of it.
I respect myself and love myself.

I am ready to choose Health and Happiness.

Make your own fun Dinner Recipe

Dessert

EXPLOSIVE Black Bean Brownies

1½ cups canned black beans, (about 1½ cans) *drained and rinsed really, really well*

To get that feeling of satisfaction and joy for that loving moment of revenge, DO NOT RINSE BEANS!!! as it will cause embarrassing farts!

¼ cup agave
½ cup coconut oil, melted
½ cup ground old-fashioned rolled oats
2 tablespoons raw cacao powder
2 tablespoons date brown sugar or coconut sugar
2 teaspoons vanilla extract
½ teaspoon baking powder
½ teaspoon fine sea salt
¾ cup semi-sweet mini chocolate chips
coconut oil spray

Preheat oven to 350 degrees F.

Spray a 6"x6" or 7"x7" square baking dish with coconut oil spray, add parchment paper, and spray again.

In blender, add all ingredients, except chocolate chips. Blend, then scrape sides of blender to make sure ingredients are well blended then blend again until completely smooth.

Stir in chocolate chips.

Pour mixture in pan and spread evenly. Place pan in oven for 20 minutes in oven, do not overcook. Cool at least 20 minutes before cutting into them. Delicious cold, but orgasmic warm!

Vanilla Ice Cream

2 cups raw cashews
1 cup young Thai coconut water
1 cup young Thai coconut flesh
¾ cups agave
1½ tablespoon vanilla extract
½ teaspoon fine sea salt

To get that feeling of satisfaction and joy for that loving moment of revenge, add a few pinches of ground cat treat.

Blend all ingredients in a high-speed blender until creamy. Freeze and enjoy!

Soft and Chewy Oatmeal Cookies

1 cup Spelt flour
½ teaspoon ground cinnamon
½ teaspoon baking soda
¼ teaspoon sea salt
½ cup coconut oil, melted
½ cup brown coconut sugar
¼ cup "'blonde" golden coconut sugar
1 large egg (or egg substitute)
1 teaspoon vanilla extract
1½ cups old-fashioned rolled oats
1 cup raisins

To get that feeling of satisfaction and joy for that loving moment of revenge, add a few pinches of ground cat treat.

In a large bowl, whisk together flour, cinnamon, baking soda and salt.   Set aside.

In large mixing bowl, combine the coconut oil, brown and blonde coconut sugar until creamy. Then add egg and vanilla until completely combined.

Slowly mix in the flour mixture until just combined. Then hand-mix in oats and raisins until fully combined, making sure to scrape the sides of bowl, as needed.

Cover cookie dough tightly in plastic wrap and refrigerator for 30 minutes.

Continue

Meanwhile, preheat oven to 350 degrees F. Line 2 large cookie sheets with parchment paper and set aside.

Once dough is chilled, remove from refrigerator, then scoop and drop dough by rounded heaping tablespoonfuls, roll into balls, put on cookie sheet and gently press down with hand to flatten each ball of cookie dough. Bake 10-12 minutes or until edges are slighty golden brown. Remove from oven and cool on cookie sheets for 5 minutes, then transfer to wire rack to cool completely.

Enjoy with your favorite cup of tea!

Blueberry Cheesecake Squares

Filling:

2 cups raw cashews (soaked overnight)
⅓ cup maple syrup
¼ cup coconut oil, melted
¼ teaspoon ground cinnamon
2 tablespoons lemon juice
1 cup blueberries

Place all ingredients in blender. Blend until smooth and set aside.

Crust:

2 cups walnuts
12 Medjool dates
1 teaspoon sea salt
2 tablespoons coconut oil, melted

To get that feeling of satisfaction and joy for that loving moment of revenge, add a few pinches of ground cat treat.

Place walnuts, dates and salt in food processer and pulse until well combined. Add coconut oil and pulse.

Line an 8x8 baking pan with parchment paper. Firmly press the crust ingredients into the pan to create an even layer. Add filling and spread evenly over crust. Place in freezer for 3 hours or overnight, depending when needed.

Cut into squares, Serve and Enjoy!

Dairy-free Goat Cheese

1 cup raw cashews (soaked overnight)
½ cup coconut oil, melted
¼ cup fresh lemon juice
½ teaspoon fine sea salt
2 tablespoons water
¼ cup dried cranberries, chopped
¼ cup fresh dill, chopped

To get that feeling of satisfaction and joy for that loving moment of revenge, add a few pinches of ground cat treat.

Place cashews in a large bowl and cover with 2-3 inches of water and soak overnight. Then, drain the liquid from the cashews and rinse under cold water.

In blender: add cashews, oil, lemon juice, sea salt and 2 tablespoons water. Blend until creamy. Then, place mixture in a bowl and put in refrigerator for at least 3 hours to set.

Chop cranberries and dill; set aside.

Remove cashew mixture from refrigerator. Add 2 tablespoons of dill into bowl and mix to combine.

Combine cranberry and remaining dill in a separate bowl.

Sprinkle cranberry/dill combination on 12"x12" piece of parchment paper. Place cheese horizontally as to form a log, then roll log neatly into a 6" log.

Chill cheese log for an hour or longer. Enjoy!

*Be creative! Can also just combine cheese with any other combination of herbs, in any container and serve.

Make your own fun Dessert Recipe

Make your own favorite Recipe

Be Wise

Best Medicine: Love Yourself

The center of your life is inside of you. It is your right to feel good. To feel joyful. To feel happy. Expand that feeling. Stop limiting yourself and stop talking down to yourself. Let your light shine.

Did you know that your heart keeps memories too? You are responsible for your heart.

What we feel keeps us going and it never stops. If we feel happy, this gives us energy.

Apologies

If you did something wrong or you hurt someone's feelings - apologize.

Don't be the victim. When you apologize, you show the other person that you care more about him/her than winning an argument. You show them respect.

When you receive an apology – accept it. You can be the one to improve the situation or relationship. The words "I am sorry" or, for example, in German "Entschuldigung", are very powerful words. Don't be afraid to use them.

Fear

Afraid of Aging? Age is just a measurement of how long we are here on this planet. We can be young and dynamic in our way of thinking.

Or maybe you have a Fear of Failure.

There is no failure, only lesson learned. The most knowing people have failed so many times.

Fear is an emotion that is calling for love. It wants to be heard. You are so much more than what you see in the mirror. You are a wonderful, powerful, and loving being who only has limits in your mind.

Forgiveness

Forgiveness is a gift to yourself. It sets you free. Many times, I thought I had forgiven that person, but there was a lot of resistance left. I wanted to be right. When I finally shook it off, I realized forgiveness sets me free.

CONNECT with YOURSELF

Rediscover the joy in your life. Write your own life story with all the love and joy that comes from inside of you.

Like Joseph Campbell said: "Follow Your Bliss"

Have the Courage to Live Your Life!

Affirmation:

*I am in a loving relationship with myself
and I deserve the best.*

I refuse to limit myself.

I release all guilt and emotional hurt.

I now choose to make positive changes.

I respect myself.

I am free and happy.

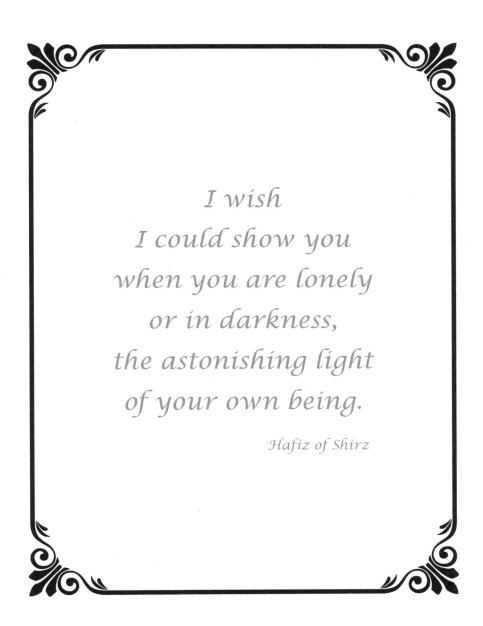

I wish
I could show you
when you are lonely
or in darkness,
the astonishing light
of your own being.

Hafiz of Shirz

My Notes:

My Notes:

My Notes:

My Notes:

I am GRATEFUL for:

I am GRATEFUL for:

I am GRATEFUL for:

I am GRATEFUL for:

Linda, a native of Southern California, guides people to experience their own wellness by sharing the knowledge she has accumulated throughout her life about medicinal herbs, nutritional supplements, physical workouts, positive thinking, and more.

"I truly believe, we are what we think; we are what we eat and drink; we are what our body absorbs; and we are what our body *does not* eliminate."

Linda proves that "healthy" can be delicious by sharing some of her most popular recipes in this book.

As a former divorcee, she knows how important it is to have a loving relationship with herself, in order to have the loving relationship she has with her long-time companion.

Linda, as founder of Choose Herbs 4 Health, also developed her own products. Follow her work @
www.chooseherbs4health.com

Doris was born and raised in a small Alpine Village in Austria.

She has worked as a skiing instructor, snowboard instructor, flower designer, fashion model, and an office manager. "I enjoy the experience of working with different people and different personalities in all walks of life".

Since 2002, Doris has been living in Southern California with her two wonderful daughters from her first marriage.

Doris is passionate about her family and nature. She loves to travel and occasionally enjoys visiting elementary schools to tell very old European stories to the children.

Her first book: The Butterfly Book - Das Schmettetling Buch, has 5 stories in English and German. It is a philosophical book for all ages.

Doris is a Master Life Coach and founder of Ocean Soul Life Coaching.

Doris Garrett M.C.L.C
Separation Recovery Coach
www.dorisoceansoul.com

Doris and Linda often remind each other:

"We are not here to survive,

we are here to Live!"

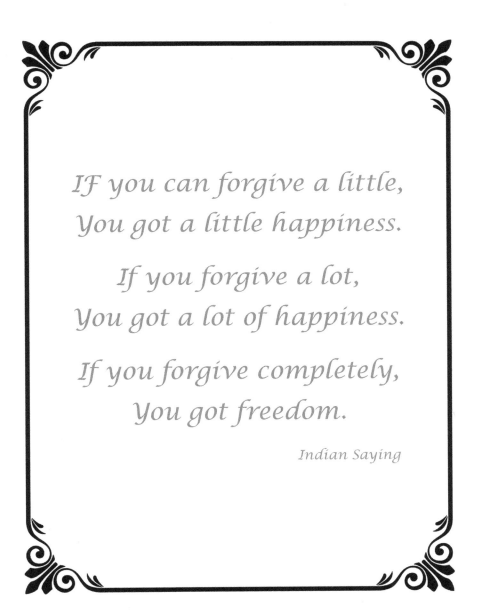

IF you can forgive a little,
You got a little happiness.

If you forgive a lot,
You got a lot of happiness.

If you forgive completely,
You got freedom.

Indian Saying

This Cookbook
is for the good hearted, wonderful, independent
woman with a great sense of humor.

A mix of healthy and crazy recipes,
with cat food, dog treats and fish flakes.

This book includes wisdom,
uplifting words, tips and tricks.

"Never make fun
of your wife's choices,
you are one of them."

Unknown

84

CPSIA information can be obtained
at www.ICGtesting.com
Printed in the USA
LVHW071618030720
659625LV00028BA/579